ALEX THE PARROT

No Ordinary Bird

by

Stephanie Spinner

illustrated by

Meilo So

Alfred A. Knopf
New York

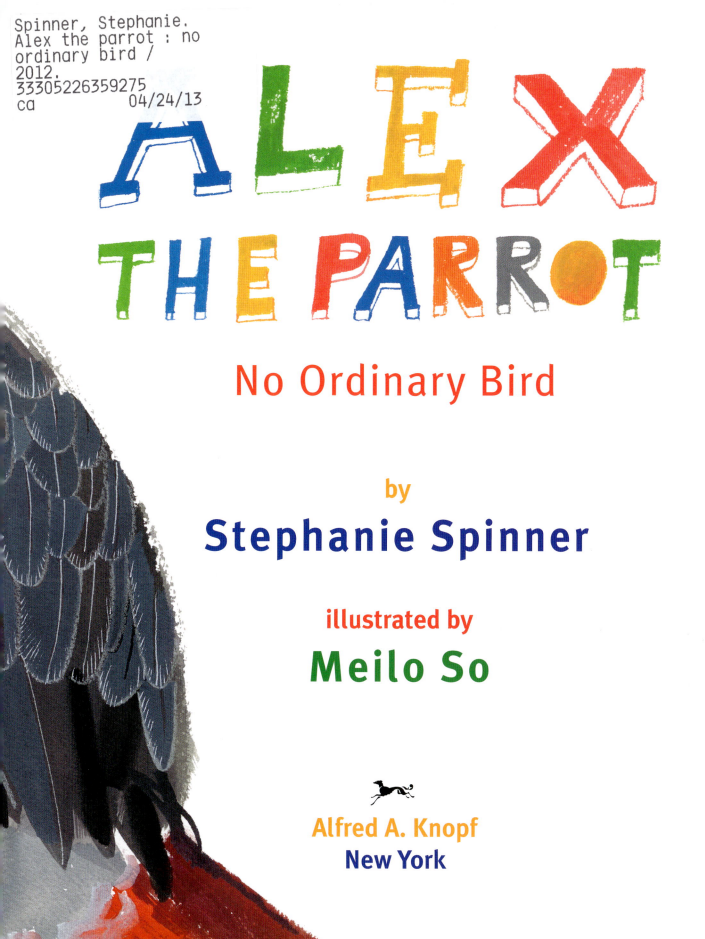

Chapter 1
Pick a Parrot, Any Parrot

One June day in 1977, a young woman walked into a pet store looking for an African grey parrot. The store had eight. They were all young birds, with bright, white-ringed black eyes, gray body plumage, and crimson tails. The woman couldn't decide which one to take, so she asked the storekeeper to choose for her.

"Okay," he said, picking the bird closest to the cage door. This grey was a year old and weighed about a pound. Singled out, he began trembling.

The woman was a graduate student named Irene Pepperberg. She made the parrot as comfortable as she could, and then began the long drive to the biology lab at Purdue University in Indiana. On the way, she decided to call her new bird Alex—short for **A**vian **L**earning **EX**periment.

Irene didn't know it then, but Alex was no ordinary parrot. He was going to make history.

Irene met Alex at a time when most people thought that animals were just barely intelligent. They could be trained to understand spoken commands, but none of them could respond with speech. The only exceptions, parrots and mynah birds, could speak words and even short sentences, but probably didn't understand what they were saying. They were only imitating, or "parroting," sounds they heard—or so most people thought.

Irene didn't agree. She had loved birds from the age of four, when she was given a parakeet for her birthday. Growing up, she had raised many pet parakeets; she had even taught some of them to talk. In her opinion, her birds were highly intelligent.

Yet studying parrots didn't occur to Irene until a few years before she bought Alex. She had been studying chemistry at Harvard and planned to teach it.

But in the winter of 1974, she happened to see a television series about a new science—the study of animal language. The shows fascinated her. One was about whales singing; another was about the sounds and gestures that chimpanzees make to each other. Most interesting of all to Irene was a show about birdsong.

The subject of animal communication drew Irene like a magnet. She began finding out everything she could about it. She read about dolphins who were learning to understand words and recognize symbols. She read about chimps and gorillas who were "speaking" with their trainers using sign language.

At the time, most scientists thought that the bigger the brain, the smarter the creature. So studies of animal communication centered on apes and dolphins, whose brain size is similar to ours.

African greys, with their walnut-size brains, were at the very bottom of the heap: "birdbrains." Nobody was interested in working with them—yet.

There are thousands of bird species. We know now that African grey parrots are among the very smartest. They are also among the most vocal. They squawk, they sing, and they love to imitate noises they hear. They can sound like just about anything.

They can also speak as clearly as people—which made an African grey the perfect bird for Irene to study.

She knew from her many parakeet pets just how intelligent birds could be. As a scientist, she wanted to prove it.

With Alex, she was determined to try.

Chapter 2

TESTING, TESTING

Alex and Irene got off to a bumpy start. Alex was frightened and unhappy in his new home in the biology lab. He wouldn't eat or come out of his cage.

Slowly, patiently, Irene helped him to overcome his fear. Within a few days, he was walking in and out of his cage and perching comfortably on her arm.

On his fourth day at the lab, Irene gave Alex an index card. He promptly shredded it with his beak. She gave him another, and another. He shredded away enthusiastically.

Each time she gave him a card, she would say, "Paper." She wanted him to understand that "paper" meant the stuff he was ripping apart.

But did he? It was too soon to tell.

Young parrots in the wild learned by imitating their parents. Parrots in captivity learned by imitation, too. But exactly what they learned, and how well they understood it, was still a question. By using a new teaching method with Alex (called the "model-rival" method), Irene hoped to find the answer.

She and a student assistant would sit in front of Alex and pretend to teach each other a word. For example, Irene would show the student a key, saying "key." The student would repeat the word "key," and Irene would hand the object over. The student would handle the key with great interest, and then show the key to Irene. When Irene responded by again calling it "key," she would get to hold it.

Then it was Alex's turn. If he said "key," he would be given the key as a reward. He liked this "game" and caught on very quickly.

Within a few weeks, Alex was saying "ee" for "key" and "pay-er" for "paper." Next he began labeling materials, such as "cork" and "wood," and colors— "green" and "blue."

Alex picked up words for his favorite foods all by himself: "nut," "banana," "corn," "grape," "cherry," and "pa," his special word for pasta. He even made up a word for apple—he called it "banerry," a combination of "banana" and "cherry."

Alex was a great student. And as he learned more words, he lost his shyness. In fact, he turned into a very bossy parrot. He let everybody know what he wanted, pretty much all the time.

"Want nut!" and "Want banana!" were two of his favorite commands. "Wanna go back" was another. It meant he was tired of working and ready for a break.

Alex made it very clear that he liked to be obeyed. If he asked for a grape and got a banana, somebody was going to end up with a banana facial.

It wasn't long before "no" became one of Alex's favorite words, too.

Alex got lots of attention, treats, and toys, every day. Yet he still got bored. And he had his own way of showing it.

He would ignore his trainers.

Or tease them by giving wrong answers.

Or throw things onto the floor.

Or chew up telephone books.

He spent most of his time with two teachers, going over the same questions again and again. He knew the answers, but he had to take the same test dozens of times.

"Alex, what color?"

"Green."

"What matter?"

"Wood."

"Alex, what shape?"

"Ball."

"What color?"

"Blue."

"What matter?"

"Wool."

Sometimes he had to take the same test fifty or sixty times.

Boring!

Irene knew Alex was bored, but her work with him required repetition. If her tests weren't absolutely thorough, they would be dismissed as "unscientific." Worse, her parrot would be called just another Clever Hans.

Clever Hans was a horse who lived in Germany more than 100 years ago. He seemed to be highly intelligent, and people flocked to see him perform.

Hans's owner, Wilhelm von Osten, would ask Hans math questions. If he asked Hans to add two and two, Hans would answer by tapping his hoof four times.

Six minus three? Three taps. Two plus three? Five taps. Hans always gave the right answer.

Von Osten believed that Hans could really add and subtract. But he was wrong. Von Osten was moving his head—very, very slightly—when Hans came to the right number. Without knowing it, he was sending cues to his horse.

Hans couldn't do math after all. But he did understand body language. Von Osten's signals were almost invisible, but Hans saw them.

Irene made sure that nobody sent cues to Alex. Many different people tested him. Complete strangers sometimes asked him questions. Even without Irene in the room, Alex got the answers right.

Chapter 3
ALEX SAYS "NONE!"

Alex began his training by learning "key" and "paper" and other single words. After about a year, he began to group words together. This was a very big step. When Alex called something "four-corner wood," he was doing something no other bird had done. He was showing that he understood numbers (four), shapes (square), and materials (wood). When he called something "green peg wood" or "blue key," he was proving that he knew colors, too.

There were chimpanzees and gorillas in other parts of the country who could understand numbers, shapes, materials, and colors also. They "spoke" with their trainers by "signing," just as some deaf people use sign language.

A chimp named Washoe could sign about 130 words. A gorilla named Koko could sign about 200.

But only Alex could understand hundreds of words—and say them.

By the time he was in his teens, Alex had learned to count up to six, to add, and to subtract.

He could say when something was bigger or smaller. He could tell what was the same and what was different.

"Alex, what's the same?"

"Color."

"What's different?"

"Shape."

"Alex, how many same?"

"Three."

"How many different?"

"One."

Alex also understood something children can't grasp until they are four or five: the concept of zero. When zero was the right answer, Alex used the word "none."

"Alex, what's different?"

"None."

These were things no chimp or gorilla could do. Alex wasn't supposed to have the brainpower to do them, either. But that didn't stop him.

Over the years, Irene wrote about Alex's amazing progress. But scientific magazines ignored her. Up until the 1980s, most scientists believed that only humans could speak and understand words.

A few scientists thought differently. One was Roger Fouts, who had begun teaching Washoe the chimp to use sign language in 1967. Another was Francine Patterson, who had been teaching sign language to Koko the gorilla since 1972.

Chimps and gorillas grow up in the wild using gestures that resemble sign language. This gave Washoe and Koko the natural ability to learn it. Even so, training them took years.

African greys in the wild often imitate the sounds of other birds and animals. As far as we know, their calls and cries don't resemble spoken language. But even if they did, teaching Alex to speak would still have been very demanding. So it is not surprising that Roger and Francine admired what Irene was doing.

After years of hard work, it was good to be taken seriously.

Chapter 4
ALEX SAYS "YOU Tickle!"

Meanwhile, stories about Alex began showing up in newspapers and magazines.

When he and Irene appeared on television, millions of people saw for themselves how intelligent he was.

The result? Alex became famous—a parrot celebrity! His fans were impressed with his intelligence, of course. But they loved him because he was a show-off—a very funny one.

He would sway and bob his head in time to music.

He would stick his head in a mug and make silly noises.

He would say, "Want a showaa," until someone sprayed him with water.

When he wanted a tickle, he would say, "You tickle!" Then he would bend his head, exposing his neck. Alex liked being tickled so much that his face would turn pink with pleasure.

When he was a little older, Alex learned a new command: "Go see tree." It meant he wanted to be taken to a window so he could watch the birds outside. He seemed to like them.

The birds inside were a different matter.

In 1995, Irene got another African grey to train. She named him Griffin. He was a tiny baby, just seven weeks old. He needed lots of special care. He had to be fed by hand, carried in a blanket, and watched closely.

Irene hoped that Alex would welcome the young bird. But on their first meeting, Alex narrowed his eyes and made an angry growling noise. Then he headed straight for Griffin, beak-first.

The message was clear: Griffin was definitely *not* welcome. Alex, and only Alex, was the boss.

In time, peace returned to the lab—as long as everybody followed Alex's rules. He was "top bird." He always had to perch higher than Griffin and closest to Irene. When she came into the lab, she had to greet him first. Otherwise, he would sulk!

When Griffin started to learn words the same way Alex had, Alex liked to butt in. He would say the right word really fast—before Griffin could. Or he would cry, "Say better!" That was his bossy way of telling Griffin to speak more clearly.

Sometimes he would even say a wrong word, just to confuse the younger bird.

Griffin was a good sport about Alex's teasing. So were the assistants who helped Irene. It wasn't always easy. They were dealing with Boss Alex, after all.

As soon as a new assistant entered the lab, Alex began issuing orders. "Want nut!" "Want grape!" "Go get dinner!" he would call. "Come here!" "Pay attention!" "You tickle!"

He showed no mercy.

Nevertheless, Alex liked the assistants a lot. Once he got to know them, he would call them by name and dance on their shoulders. He would even chime in when they sang. At those times, Alex was a very good boss.

At night, Alex would sit in his cage and talk to himself. He would repeat phrases. He would rhyme words, whistle, and caw. He would often imitate Irene. "Good parrot! Good boy!" he would say, or, "Try better. What's your problem?" He sounded just like her.

There were still people who doubted that Alex understood what he was saying, but Irene was sure that he did. She had tested him thousands of times. Besides, they understood each other. They were old friends.

On the last night she saw him, they parted in their usual way. Alex said, "You be good. I love you." Irene told Alex she loved him, too. Then he asked, "You'll be in tomorrow?"

"Yes, I'll be in tomorrow," she answered.

The next morning, Irene received an email from the lab that began, "Sadness." It went on to deliver terrible news: Alex was dead.

At first, Irene couldn't believe it. Alex was only thirty-one, and greys often live to be over sixty.

But it was true. On September 7, 2007, Alex had died in his cage of heart failure. Their long, wonderful friendship was over.

News of Alex's death flew around the world. It was reported on television and in newspapers everywhere. Even scientific magazines ran the story. Alex videos appeared daily on the Internet, and millions of people watched them. Friends, colleagues, and Alex fans from countries near and far wrote to Irene, expressing their sorrow.

Alex had touched them all. In his short life, he had made a big difference. First and foremost, he changed the way people thought about birds. He showed that they were smarter than anybody had ever dreamed. Alex was as smart as a five-year-old child. Until then, only chimps and gorillas had tested that high.

Alex also made people understand that African greys are much happier when they have company. They live in flocks in the wild, and are almost never alone. As pets, they shouldn't be alone too much, either.

And as very intelligent pets, they need to play and learn. If they don't, they get bored and misbehave, just the way children do.

After hearing about Alex, many owners changed the way they treated their African greys. Thanks to him, their pet greys now lead much better lives.

Alex
the Parrot

Irene's work did not stop with Alex. After his death, she kept on teaching African greys. Griffin became her main student, and he made great progress.

When he was twelve, Griffin took part in an unusual experiment. He went to a nursery school where the children were three, four, and five years old. He was tested on words, shapes, numbers, and colors. So were the children.

Griffin did very well. He scored as high as the three-and-a-half-year-olds.

These results were important. They proved that Griffin—or some other African grey—might turn out to be just as smart as Alex.

That may happen. But even if it does, Alex won't be forgotten.

He was the first.

A Note from the Author

I grew up with dogs. First came Ginger, a boxer who saved my life by pulling me out of the ocean when I was a toddler. Knowing this, how could I object when she draped her seventy-pound body across mine every night, as if I were a lumpy pillow put there solely for her comfort? Then came Hugo, a rather aloof miniature schnauzer who groomed himself as carefully and thoroughly as a cat. With his knowing eyes, pristine white whiskers, and measured, authoritative bark, he seemed more like a merchant banker to me than a dog. Finally there was Beau, an affable German shepherd mix who was every bit as friendly to the burglars who stole my mother's jewelry as he was to our other, more welcome visitors. Until now, I've never really asked myself why I can remember these animals so well, why they're clearer to me than so many of my relatives and childhood friends. It's partly that I spent so much time walking and feeding them, of course. More important was the time I spent alone with them, gazing into their eyes, wishing for a way to bridge the distance between us. I dreamed of achieving the rapport I had read about in books like *National Velvet, Lad: A Dog,* and *The Jungle Book.* I knew they were "made up" stories, yet I loved the idea that such communication was possible.

But what could help *me* achieve it? A spell? A charm? A magical cookie? If there was anything that could dissolve the boundaries between us, allowing Ginger to tell me why she pulled me out of the ocean, and Hugo to say why he preferred me to my siblings (was it my uncanny empathy, or simply the fact that I fed him?), I yearned for it. If you've ever wished you could talk to your pets, or wondered what they were thinking, you know exactly what I mean.

Happily, our understanding of animals has come a long way since the last century. Our attitudes have changed so much that many animals might admit that we've improved. Thanks to the brilliant work of people like Roger Fouts; Francine Patterson; and Irene Pepperberg, Cynthia Moss, Temple Grandin, and countless others, we are much closer to hearing what animals have to say, and valuing what they tell us. It's still in the future, but I like to think that one day we won't really need that magic cookie.

—S.S., October 2012

For
Janet Schulman

THIS IS A BORZOI BOOK PUBLISHED BY ALFRED A. KNOPF

Text copyright © 2012 by Stephanie Spinner
Jacket art and interior illustrations copyright © 2012 by Meilo So

Library of Congress Cataloging-in-Publication Data
Spinner, Stephanie.
Alex the parrot : no ordinary bird / by Stephanie Spinner ; illustrations by Meilo So. — 1st ed.
    p. cm.
 ISBN 978-0-375-86846-7 (trade) — ISBN 978-0-375-96846-4 (lib. bdg.)
 [1. African gray parrot—Juvenile literature.] I. So, Meilo, ill. II. Title.
 SF473.P3S69 2012
 636.6'865—dc22
 2011014381

The illustrations in this book were created on Saunders Waterford cold-press paper with color ink, watercolor, gouache and colored pencils.

MANUFACTURED IN CHINA
October 2012   10 9 8 7 6 5 4 3 2 1 First Edition